SKINNY

Carolyn Hembree

Kore Press • Tucson • Arizona

standing by women's words since 1993

Kore Press, Inc., Tucson, Arizona USA
www.korepress.org

Design by Sally Geier
Cover design by Lisa Bowden
Cover photo by Valerie Galloway
Set in Myriad Pro, Matrix Narrow, Onyx, Gloucester and Garamond Narrow. Printed in the United States
of America.

We express our gratitude to those who make Kore Press publications possible: The Tucson-Pima Arts
Council, The Arizona Commission on the Arts, through appropriations from the Arizona State Legislature,
the National Endowment for the Arts, and individuals.

   Library of Congress Cataloging-in-Publication Data
Hembree, Carolyn.
  Skinny / Carolyn Hembree.
    p. cm.
  ISBN 978-1-888553-50-5
  I. Title.
  PS3608.E473S57 2012
  811'.6—dc23
                    2012026046

if you have ever picked up an old Nehi bottle buried in a ditch
for two cents and poured the muddy water and seen a tadpole
beating his tail on the new hot mix asphalt that the prisoners
was made to lay down just the other day that stuff still crawling
over the weeds and all and you see that tadpole like the black rag
of a flag flapping on a dead mast then you know what I mean you
know what people will do to one another
—*Frank Stanford*

And then the snake of speech was stirred.
—*Heather McHugh*

for

Mamie Roberts Mummert

contents

one

You know my adventurous spirit and my desire
to live and realize the greatest thrills so that I can
describe them in a romance of adventures.

—*The Perils of Pauline* (1914, Louis J. Gasnier and Donald MacKenzie, directors)

A Real Movie Star

A killer in flat olive skins tonight inside this far-off island
dream would lean fast under a low ceiling now against the blank

bandstand then against the long wall of a basement of a long dance
hall and out his dual knifeneedle take.

            Crowd keeps while breakneck we
onto a designer street, a day wind northerly against us, us running as if

the world ought a forest be—tall and winsome and all the good
air and time and talk you could take you'd be brought.

Bird: Saw you got sick to carnival ruin, Skinny, why?
                                 Make sad.

Let envy stop at your door, not in, for head and heart's a store
robbed by the many flights of her blonde dreamy satiny head tossed back

like a real movie star enameled hugely, a face framed in
a dream by a curtain not so bright as the red,

                     red of her heart matching her dress with wintry
spots designed. This star, these rolled hills, us in stars tossing spies

her head up to a biggest box listening hard—says, Ow
asks if her ear is burned.
            Skinny: I don't say, just a little melting is.

                             Bird: You're glad by it.
Behind her, the killer in metal-burned skins (fingers and nails

around her chest) says, Come back to us and out his dual knife-
needle takes and gentle in her throat as if love were given and

last upon her face a new tool like a hairbrush electric (needles not bristles)
places until with egg speckles covers she, us sees.

Skinny: That a sad thing got in me.

                                    Bird: I swear you don't know shit, Skinny.

Skinny: And won't since my best one went all's a blue coil in me.
Bird: Not your time yet, Skinny.

Skinny's Nativity and a Bird's Quietus

1

Out of a purple bunched-up surf
out of a fluorescent ripply
shore of beach towel
swaddling, half an arm
skinnily flails.

So love
love the window, the wavy
lovey-dovey window. Each lit pore
of a bobby pinned head
on a sky pillowcase love. To pieces
Skinny, the lotioned-up, sleep-lined
cheek of longing: You wouldn't, Love-
bug, goes the Mother through capped teeth,
on us dare turn.

2

First Cousin's morning menthol

       filter waterlogged in Mamie's pink soap dish

Mamie's trash burning

       onto dead bird peach can juice slow as hot lye

Fish fry

       smoky caverns inside, out: fast dancing, holiday lights, wintry
       spotted swimsuits

Red cavern floor

       Old Sweetheart's cursive fingernail carvings along Skinny's inner thigh

Biggest Car

       Old Sweetheart: Up, up SkinnyMini! I can't open the choke!
       They're telling me New York City's an island, this beach manmade
       so we're fixing—oh Skinny!—we're fixing to dive—

Still of Mamie and Bird

Who's turned the chairs to the wall in the front room,
dreamy wall nightly dreamt up by the floor lamp?
Who's heard the whistling Bird whistle thrice?

Mamie supine in the back room   L'Air du Temps
and cherry wood, her slender carved bedposts and bed doll.

Close, the Bird whispers out—
Who wrung the necks of your hopes, Skinny?

Bird loose—wire cage turned to sand flying away,
Bird into baby grand fly, into wall, into shadow fly.
Bird in a beach towel dies like fruit dies—softer.

Orange breast feather—Red breast feather

.   .   .

Chair full of holes in the shower holds her body up,
a chair water runs through like memory and is lost.

Stand in her mirror, turn it right side out
then step into your grieving like a shift, Skinny.

The way lightning flashes inside a bright day—
the way a mother's ills take stronger in the child.

Meditation on Picasso's *Guernica*

Not the one wailing, arms raised
afore a little window
not the one wailing, arms drug down by a baby
its limp head by the bare light bulb light
seen, not these but that very light
glinting off a point run through
the Horse Head that frights us.
Oh, we'd do it different now, us would!
May we do it different now in the Indoor Forest?
Bird: Your fright is a horse Skinny, its death fulsome.

May we do it different now in the Indoor Forest?
Already land is burned and must be
burned more for us does battle to the other side,
and must blow the Indoor Forest open,
must see clean across to the enemy,
across the divide. Fighters, push
the detonator plunger down into a biggest box!
(To have done it different)
Mad-dashing to the other side to count damages
us through a hung mist goes over a ground of grid

victorious under a changing light, a body finds.
Behold the Horse Head, behold
what was ours, us has no throat to wail
reins on either side of its neck
blown open, yet no gushing just split
wire exposed, laced through the Horse
Head, pulled through the body
split wire leading to two screws atop a biggest box
detonator plunger pushed down.
How well the inside the outside belies—

wire laced through like reins internalized.
The Horse Head first says, Kiss me
—Bird: Kiss him softly, Skinny—

then says, Kiss me differently.
                              I'm a child again

knowing what's meant
inside a trailer off the freeway
where out back grasses up through water grow
one trailer's aluminum siding remembered silver.
Have you stepped from room to room in your silver shoes?
I have stepped from the high grasses up one cement block

and another, lightstepped from room to room inside
my silver shoes—paper thin
wood paneling thinks *fill me fill me with secrets*

Behold my bedroom
by the bare light bulb light seen.
Behold one head on a feather pillow—
wailing head of a young man
laid on the chest of a child into space

staring off. Remembering is
like putting a feather underneath
the skull—remembrance of trailer,
and the high hard wind to lift it. The Horse Head
says, Kiss me differently. Us goes to, but not afore he dies.
A girl who finds her lips early will never be lonesome,
will never into space stare off,
will hum to herself, will never be caught.
I am so lonesome hum

Skinny in Mamie's Fake Bear Coat Re-enacts the Matrilineal Migration from Wales

The rape o' the milkmaid begun our line:
she did not pass unseen but out o' sight
entire: 'twas olden time and almost she
made out the prickly grass, the dropp'd pail creakin' . . .

Both fists on the oily dresser, Mamie hauls herself up, says,
You're fibbing, Skinny, out from 'hind that shade!

. . . and 'cross the 'lantic from Wales, them pails swingin' . . .
Sea Captain: Ahoy! 'tis sniff o' land y'almost can see!
. . . off gangplank she skedaddle, conch to ear:
Welch Milkmaid: I cer heb g heb caerfa

Skinny's *Woo Me Woo Me* Night-Night Poems

1

Bird Bird Bird
how by nightfall
Bird come
in them orange
breast feathers
all dust-rolled
how Bird come
spaking to spaking for
me (missaying all
I's thinking) how
by Skinny Bird call
me by Skinny
all night
       nary a sound
from the back room

2

Upstairs the vanity mirror level one chill eye on me
one eye first fog over then beguile me *Fame Fame*

I nearly been beguiled
downstairs under fog by Biggest Car barely
running first sight of Old Sweetheart
sighting me by window
holler he   We all famous standing in our own mirror
boastly I   I wasn't meant for nothing no
meaning a wrinkle came betwixt me and mine
meaning him might open my yearning yes
like a suitcase them velvety ropes
undid them shifts
shook out one by one

one old passenger door open
riddled then painted badly over
(open for me) Get in

3

Once in the front room snipping Old Sweetheart's hair
my scissor blade over the scalp laying over titanium

scared of the metal plate screwed with three screws into Sweetheart's head
scared of it and the shape it give
and the skull that's been taken out and thought that needs be taken back

him reading me backwards and forwards
skinny enough front to back newsprint reads through me

me bemoaning Please you can't leave me
onto the floor into a box Old Sweetheart's tendrils sweeping
them tendrils like orange feathers there lie

4

Bird say Show it Skinny
(I could) I known a way or two
a bird can die

ever let one loose inside bandied by wall by
baby grand by ceiling and floor
ever see one stunned betwixt the pink of the light

bird eye into fish eye turns

5

Of Real Movie Star's gliding I did a bit know
up inside the hill freeway nearby
down below went the city the manmade beach
them black waters albeit unseen *glide glide*
holiday lights round caverns strung up
albeit no special time
up inside the hill Biggest Car flush to concrete wall
left running the song and high beams
beaming onto the black swimming
pool barely four feet deep
onto Real Movie Star's blond dreamy satiny head tossed back
I thought to dive in without busting my head open
I thought to swim diagonal
but Real Movie Star boastly I am the First Lady here
I learn to swim correctly by swimming diagonal
so much the legs and bodies of her (time
and again) her gliding
meantime Old Sweetheart touching them much
I be panicky head of a horse
water level rising
house floating by me bigger to bigger
them headlights flash
I crawl Get in the fucking car Skinny
his bulbous knife handle of ivory
or bone hoary and unscuffed as cheekbone
scared of it and the shape it give

6

Bird say Not your time yet Skinny

To my neck
say   Ye old gal

To eye the gilded brass hook a-
flame
in far

ceiling
corner

for hanging indoors
plant for them
draping
weepy

over the sides
into

sunlight

there be no
plant hung
up by brass

brassy curls of vanity chair back in
far room corner

white vinyl

cushion of the seat that spin

stepping up to it

stepping onto it   wobbly

stepping off into   lightflies

spinning then dusting round my skull like getting up

                                                            too
                                        quick
                                                    brass

hook yanked

down

white ceiling

dust onto

me buzzing
buzz

Skinny Versifies on the Mother in Midfall

Got a shot o' her: one hand
        thrown way up
hi ho silver 'way!
        wobblin' on pointy rocks
sigh in glee all, for she do not fall!
        who'd e'en know her now:
day in and out leaves
        scuttle whilst elevators ride
she keep the courtyard in her eye: fountain
        of a French girl wavin'
muscadine vine wind round
        a hand biddin' sailors
hither or thither, *bienvenue sailor*
        moonin' o'er this one
or that, water gush with pennies

        alright, wish on't if you like
plink: think 'fore you wish . . . hmm
        go back to her tall 'gainst
riverfronts dancehalls nightclubs shindigs
        we singin' her mind
fie meantime on the ice plates
        clinkin' round the French girl!
reach reach: a fine-tooth comb
        from the dresser slip to clatter
watch: the Mother will her shawl slip
        flimsy golden-threaded
o'er the shoulder o' thought, bare
        shivery, so you can't tell
the skin beneath from what's been laid atop

Peace on Earth Word Problem and a Bird Voiceover

If Skinny's headspace is decreased by 2h 25m of Bird talking 90 to nothing at the same time that Mamie's front room is increased by the 15 mph figure eights of a television Elvis figure skater and the 40 chews per minute of the Mother in a half-slip crunching ice and holding the 2 ft wide screen door half open and letting in no more than 1 pin oak leaf, might Skinny run into limelight or be left bereft to melt in toto into Mamie's settee?

Bird: Pinch, pinch
when you gonna grace
kelly the silver screen, huh?
Aw, *shitty shitty* you without us.

Fixing Our Bone Straight Hair for a Sunday Night Date

Kissyface

kissyface

in her three-way mirror

Menthol

in the soap dish

Both fists

on the oily dresser

Mamie hauls herself up, says, You
you're a Sunday through Monday girl

Pig

The pig's hindquarters flip-flopped;
a cane, finger's length, into its vagina slid.
Meet its eye; your fear to the wayside dropped.

Incinerator some fifty feet off; the pig stops. You opt
it to get under your skin or not. Off the pig's side,
a quarter flips (I win) then onto the dirt flops.

Pigs hate the shine. My Exacto barely lifts up
the pig's hide. By the truck bed, change the blade.
It meets my eye; my fear to the wayside dropped.

Wondrously, the pig yet rubs snout and sloped
head into ground. We have unmade.
The pig's hindquarters flip-flopped.

Beat the pig to marshmallow. Its breath: interrupt.
I skin. You cane. You can't tell, with the naked
eye, cane from cane's shadow onto a pig's side dropped.

Fifty minutes: its blinking eye to the side dropped.
I am ashamed of my family.
Into the hedge, I, the pig's hindquarters flopped.
Meet my eye; fever ribbons to the wayside dropped.

Skinny's Plan When the Mother—Her Lemon Plaid Shorty Bathrobe Half Open—Lost Her Head (Heartache of Brain Waves Heartache of Bobby Pins Rippling)

I. Gonna make every gal die to be me
      (a) take it all a little like a joke
      (b) keep Bird under wraps
      (c) get famous
      (d) do Bird in
II. Going to
        III. Going to
            IV. 'til it takes

Bon Voyage Skinny: First Cousin Advises Our Heroine to Ride Shotgun for Her Virtue

Hold
hold right there
OK uh
see my-my-my thumbs
like that
If I was to push
see I mean uh
even you   ha
little as you are
uh
could kill some guy big guy
mess with y-y-y-you

See
you push hard in

Huh

I won't
  j-j-j-

                    j-   j- -

                                                            just

hard as you can
I mean (if you can't knee him in the nuts)
ha Push hard
right through the brain See I read
I read there ain't no skull bone so the brain shoots out the other side Uh

uh

if I was to push uh   in

right
now
you-you-
you'd die
(Youcandothatdie(dieinstantaneously))

Uh
Alright
I wouldn't hurt you
Heh   heh   Skin-Skinny

                                                    (sh-sh-sh-sh-shoot right out uh onto
the other side)

                              Ifyouwanttokillamanyoupushhardin

A Couple of Odes on Her

1

Why the nightly glassful yet teeters atop her nightstand there
where us put it some time past—
us padding through the back room
all done up in heels and hairs and gasps—
the corner of Mamie's Singer machine bumping
which is sharp and shaped like a hammerhead,
is black with letters golding, is gasping back *aha!*
About-face!

Sooner or later one might answer the knife blade slicing the screen door.
Sooner or later one might about-face here in her doorframe
leaving Mamie therein without even so much as a *there, there.*
Scratchy through the whitely curled ironwork of the screen door
and there is even more collusion here—crab grass through the sidewalk.
And over there—some six or more rosebushes untooled
and roseless. Mere hours from January, leaving
Mamie therein. About-face, you all! That's all. Naw
to the twitch, to the sleep face of Mamie needling us, naw. Naw
December. Yon the pruners by a nail in the shed shall hang all season.

On to the New York New Year bash thickly in bucket seats.
Permit gargantuan lights and brass music in
in speaking good riddance to the wood and to the mead
skyrocketing past
the pink flecked stones that do glitter out from Mamie's house.
Ah Mason us has surmised, if for a split second only,
flying at top speed by, the goodness of Your design
and guessed what might be reckoned ill in us.
Patriotic the brass players play underneath
a narration from the dashboard only us hears
and a ping of the bell marking each word (believe if you will)—

A herd of them has come to the place that is a church sometimes, and they have brought folding
chairs into this place for it is packed. And Mamie has arisen and taken center stage. She is not

addled at all. She is walking on the altar. Because of her walking, she is tall. She asks the lights to dim. Then she tells how her husband made fire. Mamie arcanes—Here ydy fel my g maken fire. Aeth went 'r mead into 'r brennau. My g brung 'r brennau back . . .

Hullabaloo and balloons say *enough*
of you tipping leaky up into smoke
or clouds meaning rain for the leaves
show their backs tonight.
And us is standout clubbing in backless dresses
(Manhattan doesn't look half-bad in a dress).

Skinny: Him wanting me to want him.
Bird: You'd give your eyeteeth for a chance at that,
all brigady and all done up. Nobody's
studying you, Skinny!

Out from the wild of lights, some couples
into the corners slipping not caring if they're caught
for each corner in a room can mean contrition.
The speakers on the wall playing halfhearted
though the din of a tin drum is never far off from us—

Mamie is in a large bathing place and a broom to clean it out is against the wall. She is pressing her forehead to the tiles. There appears a redheaded woman we do not recognize. She goes to smothering Mamie with water like quicksand and her body is sheening in the water and the smallest Christmas tree atop baby grand is the same silver and she struggles very little.

By and by, the wall above her mantle might begin to crack
as the leaves are showing their backs
and if 'twere not for the rain that keeps us back
if 'twere not for the morphine patch to her flanks sticking
if 'twere not for the pinkness of the ileum exposed
if 'twere not for the hat fur-lined matching the once
reds of Mamie's hair and touched off by pink rhinestones
shaping the shape of a bird, plumes streaming upwards

and tough chunks of marcasite and pearls from the dresser strung
if 'twere not for these and the three white dogs
in her yard, pretending themselves still alive
us would say, Us loves you you can't be dying on us
who'll speak the old speak who'll speak for you—Gaaah—

2

Guilt—is Sorrow—thinking—

two

You are in the Garden of Lonely Children, in

The Tell-tale Forest of Dreams. Here things

appear as they really are.

—*The Poor Little Rich Girl* (1917, Maurice Tourneur, director)

Old Sweetheart Slams White Russians and Mudslides on Ditmars Blvd., Astoria

First words out of my mouth he say: My, my, you're not from around here.
Every bone cry *hie you hence* but in uniform he's out of this world.
Brass chicken hawk on brick wall exposed read fifty degrees.
Truly, I want a shortcut to the innermost workings of one other.

Says: You take your chances running night operations. I say goddamn.
Bird's eye view of his fingers spread out on his crown, flesh
wound. Through three shot glasses the waitress' fingers loop.
Clappin' off the beat he guffaw: You dance like a country girl. Flush.

To the beaten path of his hand in the pile of my skirt go
towards the southernmost row houses, turn at the spicy restaurant
its awning ruffling—there one woman lends another her rabbit fur.
Dream a man at the N station at the crack of dawn to sing and flaunt.

Now whether to sing or tell it other ways.
Leastways, atop the gratings a man dance with a puppet life-size
its arms to his waist tied. Hot little number, he say and has it
say *caramba* while the train skates in and speakers crackle live.

My sheets snapped flat and train-case crammed,
I never answered you (losin' your mind, scramblin' in the grass down)
asking me years hence: Why don't you sound now like where you're from?
No, you just looking hard at me—the voice is from elsewhere thrown.

Another Meditation on Picasso's *Guernica*

Horse Head blossoms in

a village scene: gold footpaths
to golden huts unwind
against the glossy red sky of the skin-
tight dress us slinks in

pose a little this way, Bird says
Skinny: GeishaSkinny now
                    ManhattanSkinny now

sliding right hand up doorframe
sideways cocking the left leg, the slit
rips a bit, well-nigh all
filaments blinking . . .
brighten:
          this club's dynamite! wow!

collects us first: wipe the brow
mount the uneven stair: swinging
open the stall to Skinny squatting
tattoo on her temple
all out of sorts: rhinestone strap
                    off the shoulder, flashy

mildew as the wet season lags on

your booth us skwunches
red vinyl to the leg sticking
sprig of pink at the shoulder
pinned droopy . . .
                    lol:
hornsman:
          da-da-da-di-da-da-da-da-da-
overhead a Horse Head
mounted as if 'twere antlers

from it growing inside the wall-
to-wall mirror, there
in the glass table top, there
in the hornsman's brass
the great teeth jutting
the Horse Head wincing:
                    do you know me?

giddap!
            heels into flanks dug
us hurls dynamite bombs into
the midst of the Indoor Forest
then high tails it!
forward! but where?
and who is the dispensator?
forward! but one approach
and the bridge is sizzling!
and sharp shooters zing ahead!
take the farthest beach, us the closest
swords drawn, tassels streaming
Horse neck veiny straining, tongue out
tail plaited and flying up
whoa there whoa Horse
taking the shrapnel blossoms
in . . .
            Christ what is this?
run under the scaffolding
                        duck! ow!
for a towel, wrap like a turban the dressing

if we can't save, the least we can do is lessen

the ssszzpow
                da-da-da-di-
over the horsepistol (ha!)

an orderly turns the Horse:
Horse Head gasping
weight on one hip
bed linens to the neck
climbing
         -da-da-da-da-da- (4/4 time)
meantime air raid siren climbs:
                              wohohohooo—

[kr]take your bird down to that island pronto, pilot![kr]
[kr]sir![kr]
the goggle band pinching us
streaming 100 mph biplane
bellows: [kr]can't guess the bla—posit—[kr]
[kr]—en—enths cloud[kr]
[kr]pot shots here[kr]
[kr]—ist[kr]
—[kr]—
[kr]losin—you[kr]
this is your number one ace chop it up fat cats! Bird hollers
[kr]roger wilco[kr]

2500 above sea level
us devil may care

                         drops all ten

see: the boulder from which water is gushing
see: hillock and sage beyond
do you recognize a face out of the face peeping?
from the island you have been trying so long to reach
from the island you have been so long out of reach

us comes nose-to-nose, land almighty!

with the Horse Head
razzmatazz of the flak of the brouhaha outside

chained to the bed
gums receding (aw) bites out
us explains:
                'twas the job you know
there be no high ground ear alway to ground, thinks Skinny
what will you squirrel away? Horse asks
as if life on it depends . . .
                      who knows

da-da-da-di-da-da-da-da-da-

off the music,
             go to the window:
of seeing your own bomber's shadow over the target
of civil war
of courthouse cobbled, columns only
of the one gulping from the hole, a mule dead beside

Skinny on the Stage

With care
slip from
the raked
stage free

Manhattan's
but a scrim

Bird Tells How It Went with Skinny's Beloved

Sh, Bird say from his clock tower
thus twitter nor tweet be heard all night
wide, drafty them halls orange feathers swoosh through
Bird: Old Sweetheart talks to hisself nowadays
he thinks nowadays he be judging crime
(seen on court steps, seen midday ranting)
Bird: He lives nowhere now you know!

I know
I picture him: Sweetheart's always to me
an oil painting—bluely plush knickers
crop in hand, too young to ride the mead
'hind him a *whinny* or *neigh* or *brrr*
'hind him a horse alights, it has wings
all things live long enough they get wings
alas! I and he be what? fly-by-night
tonight old snow outside courthouse
caught in dogwood branches

From on high seems they be blossoming
by park's spiky gate latch near froze
a girl jogs the square her dog crimson-
collared be white it be late nearby
bronze horseman his right hand free spots her
Yaah now! she hears she falls she falls
snow drifts and snowy tufts drift up

Who done it? 'twill be in court in short
order: the judge be in the clock tower
Bird: Order —everafter hurray down
down in tunnels with have-nots, has-beens
with them Old Sweetheart live this way
achoo! 'neath the courthouse 'neath pink sheets
Bird say, Boohoo
yank courthouse to close
ne'er be I whispery to him, It
be ok be ok ok o

Skinny's Ars Poetica

Going to reach down inside me
betwixt them cage wires palm down

going to find out what's down there what's rustling round
going to pull it out then look at it up close

lest I forget who ye be
hold it up to the provincial light for all to see

you know the love the love of dwelling inside another
know the peace of an orange-breasted bird

sitting atop a horse's muzzle sitting wings folded in
all them pinks of flowers round the bridle flowering

Ode on Another Ingénue's Ophelia for Two Voices

Skinny:
time to   stand the brightness of corals   rubrum   surf bumps
& blows not away   coiling Bird in place of
me I would not end to end be   stood in Real Movie Star's   splashed red taffeta

Bird:
for I splashed
it parachuting to her she shooed me leaping   herself in
dignity   is belle synchronization

Skinny:
hell or high water I'd play her   flew me out twice
to read   my face rolled   'hind the screen

Bird:
sasaki bush   reddened at winter you are   Real
there   are   5   flowers   3   crinkle

Skinny:
to heart took it
hark   Bird's an orange   blossom felled 'mong

tongues won't move on own again

The Goner

They'll read something like it somewhere—
wronged one longed all along for the long gone wrong one

wool over this one's eyes, steel wool
in that one's mouth, a half-eaten blood orange

on the floor of some abode, some dust
devil of angel dust, where, half-senseless

in a half-slip, a drama mama fans herself
with an automatic, strung along

by this mind reader, that peter
meter, another string bikini'd string bean

who in a string of bad language unstrung
my mind—a gripe a gulp a growl a glint a goring

When I Consider How My Light Is Spent

I see chandeliers of light church your living
room. I was wrong to go—don't be sore at me,
don't play possum—give me a month I'll be
home. Sleepless, tug the double-knotted string,
trip up those lightweight stairs   my way of going
comes and goes. High and low to hunt your body,
sponge diaphanous hips, your lip injury—
Christ, who mashed you under thumb? I was wrong.
A woman down the way from you was robbed.
Scrambling up stairs, her temple shot (for kicks)—
We have the money! she'd said—baby under
her torso. It lived that kind of God-awful.
I left to get famous—to hand you keys, say,
Your new lease on life. Dandelion, you fluff off.

And the Twelve Gates Were Twelve Pearls

Mamie's whitely
curled ironwork screen door
latched to
sliced ope

How My First Cousin and I Would (He Digs, I Cover) Bury the Hatchet in the Manmade Beach at Oak Mtn. St. Park

Mamie's north and east of the jetty by a yard, maybe
two. My first cousin and I swill beer, keeping an eye on
her red suit. Against the jetty stones,
white water blurs; I can't keep the elements
straight.   Waves then swims faster
as if she were younger—*Mamie.*
To make out her face, I shade mine. I don't.
Floundering now backwards—no, facedown;
Mamie's—*go*—in riptide.
                                    Midstride, my first cousin dives;
his can left on a fender or hood. I hold mine.
His hands hit the bottom. Scraped up—
Go.
Her suit-skirt isn't still, though she's.
                                    15 yards:
double-armpit tow against the current.
Her mouth slack. Her strap down.
Breaker over his head; spray on my leg.
He can't kick hard enough to ventilate her.
Breaker over his head. Spray on my leg.

The pavilion cement around her
head darkens the way shadow would.
It's noon.
I open her airway; her back align.
You're soaked to the bone—
which one?—
                    My first cousin,
out of breath, kneels by me in the sand.
Mamie's chin lifted, I take the two breaths —*try*
the dent in her breastbone.
                          15 compressions:
my shoulders align and my fingers don't touch her.
The third cycle.

Until Her Shadow's on the Curtain Round Her Bed

My whole body's a hand up inside the hole of some lacquered clock reaching—

What word or other have you now she's in her tracks stopped,
what more than *slow up for me, hey? Ta ta*
goes the rivulet that runs inside, inside this hospital partition.

You are indoors though her hand is colding. It is the South,
though she's of northern lights, of rivulets, of yellow flight,
of gases of light at some odd 40,000 degrees, say.

Do't—pile her yellow dresses at the foot of her bed!
Already her room's of light beams—
whoosh—whilst her shale grimace (catty-corner mine) stays.

My face, it cannot want to be kind.

A nurse in bouncy shoes verifies, This is no catnap and
What's worse and As you please and Moreover.
The partition. And curtain. A fluorescent strip casts her.

Like she's merely 'gainst a screen thrown, though I
her chin in one hand cup, in the other her tender spine.

For she was old—pant-
on-steps-old one mumbled once (the earpiece
not to her ear) as she always did: Such as it is . . .
Gingerly, gingerly up in arms, into her a tiny blow.

three

Then - the woman in her died and she

became a Thing . . .

—*Stella Maris* (1918, Marshall Neilan, director)

Pastoral

Tell me—for crying out loud—how at 500 fathoms that'd flower here?
Flame Creeper knotting at one's hip bone, th'other's knee.

Something's to it. Foam in an eye corner (his, hers, mine);

bubbles beading through one's bottom teeth.
Those lips fixed; these a hair apart.

Anybody'd want to reach inside his cheek.
Any'd want to tuck a pinky inside his cheek

to see —*are you here*— are you plasterwork done like flesh?
are you shale? are you
                              flesh? Oceans 'part.

Her: Goner, I can't get o'er—sweatin' him out in the crook o' my arm,
dabbin' with kerchief tip his hairline, his either eye—

him under eiderdown at the prow glintin'.
Him: You can be made to be as you was moments ago, can't you?

                    eiderdown—reverse— *eiderdown*

Enterlude danced emptyheaded with torso

Some—I—set eyes (whose?) on the notched petal, the spur at her
knee that cannot unbend, that can flower in colder springs under glass.

Just like that.
She chatters.

I set eyes on him.
He on an old jay stopping, tail feathers up. Squint: a quaver keeps it.

Her sideways in the chair, a side of her face lit.

Him one arm pushing up from the table top; its leg and hers against his.

Her the whole whole of her face

lit. Flower here. There's a pasture. The clapboard claps. The dovecote crackles. Our stables orange. They cave.

      the portal porthole

Him: I shifted my weight back and forth—you could tell I was mad—

Her: All's to gush. Thusly, nuzzle up.

The Venus de Milo Tree

Characters:

        Young Mamie, 17
        A Soldier, Young Mamie's lover
        Mamie, bedridden matriarch
        The Narrator, Mamie's caregiver
        The Venus de Milo Tree, a lovers' tree on the homestead
        Roan, a horse

Settings:

        A pastoral homestead
        A foreign shore

~ Oh cruel goddess of love! Young Mamie returns her soldier's gift. ~

Young Mamie,
flushed neck up,
snatches
the briolette
from her throat.

The Venus de Milo tree,
its canopy of leaves
memorized,
rustles
in the wee hours.

Stock-still
the perennials.

The beds
wintered-over.

~ The Lost Soldier ~

Cleft from his unit, the love story goes, he backtracked, refitting his boot, heel-toe, into his tracks silently for the drifts be like skin on this foreign front, a face in mind, in his pack the briolette she threw at him, a tooth from the front, all day (the rest of his days) going towards his own back, towards before it turned on them.

He sees two others (but he himself does not) drop. The bucket of herring filled to its lip where the top one (not flipping anymore) is kissing. The ice melted half down. A GI dropped. How did they fight so quiet-like? Pinching the lobes between his index and thumb harder until blood's to surface, propping his M1C higher on the rock, he knows this ain't no popgun, knows to clear the platform. *Don't crouch, don't make a pebble move, not a dust or there'll be smoke coming out your ears ere long.*

Concussion/fragmentation grenades. A piece in his left shoulder. *Gooks, gauze, glucose, trash fish, kimchi, ration of peas, an arm and a leg, whatever else we snuck. Shit, just go*—the wind knocks him down. Skating Hill 931 on his hands. Better: skipping rocks to cross it. Better: skipping rocks across it. But eyes saran-wrapped, he busts ass all over. His tooth chipped on a GI's tooth. Leave the GI in the drifts. He'll keep.

~ Time and Space Collapse!
(as our narrator and soldier battle the elements) ~

A soldier in my dream:
a puffed-up knuckle
through them driving gloves
driving a scraper
over the windshield,
dumping a bucket,
driving a scraper,
the drifts hither and yon . . . .
Us jimmying [rupture] a truck handle.

First killing frost
you can't with a brogan
with a steel toe
with a spade—
hell no!—
break.

~ Details for Fortifying a Winter Tree ~

November, use 10-gage galvanized steel to wire Venus from tree-rats, inch your way up from the roots to make it last until the north side where the bark's gone thick and if it's damn cold get an old sheet to drape it.

~ Intermission: (you know Mamie was always the toast of every evening) ~

The chain spread-eagle, the briolette's million faces making little lights on the walls—

A fistful of bone meal won't help. It won't help us, Venus.

There's a spot I carved you'll never spot!

At her throat (where the briolette would go) twist and pin a rosette.

Gentle Reader, what are ladies' hands for? Why, for playing gospel and setting spit curls!

Don't wire and drape a tree to look like a god and a woman.

Hands too for handing down handmade heirlooms and for keeping faces soft and new (buttercream is best).

Don't try and put a head on nature.

A briolette, a mind on the wing—

Lost you lost in this lost that you see that you got that you and that you in that

~ "The joke was on me" ~

This roan just makes out the cardinal of my laces.

You know how I come to find out I was color blind, horse blind more like. Navy wouldn't have me. Korea come, come to see I'm on the front line. I could see things the others couldn't. The joke (his shelled shoulder) *was on me.*

~ Mamie daydreams of springtime ~

Mamie's face gone
                    from babyish to serious, miniscule under her comforter. Weeks now
the right one (her side that works) sliding around under the comforter, crinkling the bed
pad. Were she to grab the dresser to stagger up.

Draw it on the sawmill walls. A circle, five feet in diameter, of skin and liquid on the
linoleum. Our roan under a blanket spins and spins on its side to stagger up. Pull the glove
off by your teeth run your fingers over the spotty coat, the spine, the sacroiliac joint, hip
joint, all jutting. The leg's broke. Fast, get under it. Gripping the cabinet door for leverage.
The roan's throat on our jeans, its skin pulled shiny, mouthing like it were bitted,
Who's the martyr here?

                              There's a nest in the lowest branch of the Venus de Milo tree.

~ I've always been fascinated by the secret life of horses ... ~

you see for once everything one   eye on the fence
one on the horizon jump   your abdomen and front   legs swimming jump
on   tiptoe your shadow   does not show you   tremor   jump   gimme
a minute   jump   your ears pinned back fly   throw your head
to the side keep the tree   limb in focus the wooden   beams
slam your ribcage   the fence posts going to pieces half boards splinters flying fifteen
feet or more behind as if they were detonated from underneath   your gums
pulling back begin getting dry   the hock joint under a bunch of boards
crisscrossed on your side
heave   heave

~ A body's not a wristwatch to unwind itself ~

A briolette, a mind is on the wing—

The sap does not rise
Mamie does not rise.
Leaves do not turn.
Venus' cells messed up.
Mamie's cells messed up.
In the small of her back
they split.

Her pillowslip,
glossy pink, burst
so the feathers
a collar make.

Sheets tangle
at her hip.
And she is wound up again.

And a body's not a wristwatch to unwind itself.

~ And the planet of Love is on high
        Beginning to faint in the light that she loves
           On a bed of daffodil sky ~

Bend the wire
where you carved *Venus*.

Her left eye shut,
her left lips pulled,
the right screwing up,
I guessed she'd dwindle.

I'd guessed wrong.
All eight feet of her
sets to rise.

Mouth open,
the soldier,
done ratting,
on his knees,
looks over his blindfold.

You mistook this grove—
               far for home.

NOTES

"And the Twelve Gates Were Twelve Pearls" —This title is from Revelation 21:21.

The Venus de Milo Tree —The last intertitle is from Tennyson's "Maud," lines 857-859.

ACKNOWLEDGMENTS

Many thanks to the editors of the publications in which the following poems previously appeared:

Antennae: "Another Meditation on Picasso's *Guernica*"
Archipelago: "Until Her Shadow's on the Curtain Round Her Bed"
Copper Nickel: "Peace on Earth Word Problem and a Bird Voiceover," "A Real Movie Star,"
    and "Skinny's Nativity and a Bird's Quietus"
The Cream City Review: "Still of Mamie and Bird"
CutBank: "Pig"
Faultline: "How My First Cousin and I Would (He Digs, I Cover) Bury the Hatchet in the Manmade
    Beach at Oak Mtn. State Park"
Forklift, Ohio: "Pastoral"
Gulf Coast: "The Goner"
jubilat: "Old Sweetheart Slams White Russians and Mudslides on Ditmars Blvd., Astoria"
Lush: A Poetry Anthology and Cocktail Guide: "Old Sweetheart Slams White Russians and
    Mudslides on Ditmars Blvd., Astoria" (reprint)
Meena: "Meditation on Picasso's *Guernica*"
New Orleans Review: "Skinny's *Woo Me Woo Me* Night-Night Poems"
Omnidawn blog: "Bird Tells How It Went with Skinny's Beloved"
Ostrich Review: "When I Consider How My Light Is Spent"
Poetry Daily: "Old Sweetheart Slams White Russians and Mudslides on Ditmars Blvd.,
    Astoria" (reprint)
Puerto del Sol: "A Couple of Odes on Her"
Thermos: excerpts from *The Venus de Milo Tree*

Thanks to Lisa Bowden and Ann Dernier of Kore Press.

Thanks to my readers—Jonathan Padgett (aka "Goat") who shared the yellow submarine;
Jane Miller who said *yes*; the late Steve Orlen who made me prove him wrong; Barbara Cully;
Brad Richard; Kay Murphy; Peter Cooley; Andy Young; Jennifer S. Davis; David McMahon;
Emily Wright; Usen Gandara; Jay Hopler; Jake Adam York; Frances Sjoberg; Forrest Gander;
Ed Skoog; Andy Stallings; Melissa Dickey; Chris Chambers; Julian Billups; Jesse Seldess;
Boyer Rickel; Anne Gisleson; Michael Tod Edgerton of "Todolyn;" and my father who left me
music and words—*It's cut and bleeding, Dad . . .*

Lynda Woolard

Carolyn Hembree has poems out or forthcoming in *Colorado Review, Gulf Coast, Indiana Review, jubilat,* and *Witness*, among other journals and anthologies. Her poetry has received three Pushcart Prize nominations, a PEN Writers Grant, a Southern Arts Federation Grant, and a Louisiana Division of the Arts Fellowship Award in Literature. Before completing her MFA, she found employment as a cashier, housecleaner, cosmetics consultant, telecommunicator, actor, receptionist, paralegal, coder, and freelance writer. Carolyn grew up in Tennessee and Alabama. She teaches at the University of New Orleans.

standing by women's words since 1993

As a community of literary activists devoted to bringing forth a diversity of voices through works that meet the highest artistic standards, Kore Press publishes women's writing that deepens awareness and advances progressive social change.

Kore publishes the creative genius of women writers to maintain an equitable public discourse and to contribute to a more diverse, and accurate, historic record.

Why we publish women:
- Since its inception in 1923, *Time Magazine* has never had a female editor.
- Since 1948, the Pulitzer Prize for Fiction has gone to 42 men and 16 women.
- Of the 108 Nobel Prize Winners in Literature, 12 have been women. Three of the 12 female winners were in the last decade.

If you'd like to purchase a Kore Press book or make a tax-deductible contribution to the vital project of publishing contemporary women's literature, please go here: **korepress.org**.